1

The Dictionary Obscura

By Sabrina Godlewski

Table of Contents

A Forward of Obscurities

When I sat down to write the Dictionary Obscura's contents, I had no idea of the amount I would learn about the English language. Originally, I started writing the dictionary to be just that: a dictionary. I enjoy collecting obscure words, and over some years, I have curated a good collection just waiting to be put together. As I did this, I started exploring obscure grammar, punctuation, and linguistic facts about the English language.

The rabbit hole I fell down was deep.

I'd like to explore the so-called *Sapir-Whorf Hypothesis*. This 'hypothesis' states two theories, one called linguistic determinism and one called linguistic relativity. Gistly, linguistic determinism (LD) and linguistic relativity (LR) can be defined like this:

- Linguistic Determinism: the concept that language and its structures limit and determine human knowledge and thought. This is considered the "strong" form of Linguistic Relativity, which is defined as:

- Linguistic Relativity: the principle that the structure of a language influences its speakers' worldviews and cognition, especially in reference to how languages shape the perceptions of the world of the speaker.

These two might seem very similar. LD states that language *determines* thought and that linguistic categories influence cognitive categories directly. Generally, LD is considered untrue by linguists in favor of the "weaker" LR, which states that linguistics shape and influence speaker perception without strictly limiting or obstructing these perceptions. "Strong" and "weak" here refer to the rigidity of the arguments.

There is a whole depth here to dive into. For our purposes, I believe it is important to lend some credence to the idea that the language we speak directly influences how we see the world, and how *well* we speak the language directly influences how *well* we understand the world around us.

In George Orwell's *1984*, "newspeak" is

implemented by an authoritarian government that has stripped "dangerous" words like *freedom* and *revolution* from the colloquial and literal dictionary. In doing so, they removed these words from society as a whole, and with them, the very *concepts* of things such as freedom or revolution. The more refined, constrictive, and reduced the language gets in the novel, the less people have to work with to understand the world around them, which is what The Party wants.

This directly ties into the *Sapir-Whorf Hypothesis*, and explains fairly clearly the purpose of the Dictionary Obscura. Though the Dictionary Obscura isn't comprehensive in capturing *every* obscurity of the English language, it *does* act as a springboard into the amorphous gray-zones of the language that we speak.

It is important to expand our linguistic vocabulary and understanding of grammatical layouts within our sentence structures. If we view language as rigid, simple, and deterministic, we limit ourselves in our understanding of the concepts that influence our lives on a day-to-day basis.

Therefore, I encourage all readers of the Dictionary Obscura to continue to branch out into the lesser known parts of English. Be they words, grammar, punctuation, concepts, or something else, it is important to have a grasp on the lesser known parts of the language in order to have a grasp on the lesser understood parts of our lives.

Onto the technical parts:

This Dictionary is established in several pieces:

1. Part One: The Dictionary Proper
    1. Obscure Words, with definitions and etymologies, broken into:
        1. Obscure Adjectives
        2. Obscure Nouns
        3. Obscure Verbs
    2. Suggested Words
2. Part Two: Obscure Grammar
    1. Obscure Grammar and Grammatical Rules
    2. Miscellaneous Obscurities

Some of these words came from lists online, some came from my own day-to-day experiences, and some came from me specifically picking through a complete, unabridged dictionary in the hunt for words. Each word has a definition, a set of synonyms and antonyms (for words that have them (unique words have a U next to them)), and the etymology of the word.

After that comes the suggested words section, which is composed of psuedowords that are proposed not only to cover niche, wordless concepts, but also to explore how to *create* words via etymology.

From there, the Dictionary branches into obscure grammar, such as Garden Path Sentences, Donkey Sentences, Split Infinitives, and more. Within each of these concepts, other concepts are explored and defined at the end of the section. This is *not* a comprehensive list of grammatical obscurities, but it is a great place to start.

Finally, there are the miscellaneous obscurities, such as the interrobang, which doesn't quite fit into any other section within this dictionary yet which still has grammatical purpose and obscurity around it.

This is not a large dictionary, nor is it comprehensive, but it is my hope that the Dictionary Obscura inspires people to explore the far reaches of the English language and pioneer new understandings of how the language works.

Not only is this fun; it is helpful, necessary even. The more one understands about their language, the more they can utilize it to express themselves and understand the world around them. This *is* the point of language, and the Dictionary Obscura exists for that sole purpose.

The more you know, the more you know.

"The job of the linguist, like that of the biologist or the botanist, is not to tell us how nature should behave, or what its creations should look like, but to describe those creations in all their messy glory and try to figure out what they can teach us about life, the world, and, especially in the case of linguistics, the workings of the human mind."

– Arika Okrent, Linguist and Author

Addendum: most of the etymologies within this dictionary come from the online etymolgy dictionary, so many thanks to that website, which can be found here: https://www.etymonline.com/

Part One:
The Dictionary Proper

Adjectives

Aberrant:

deviating from the usual or natural type; straying from the right or normal way

Synonyms:	abnormal; strange; weird; atypical
Antonyms:	normal; usual;

Etymology: from Latin *aberrantem* (nominative *aberrans*), present participle of *aberrare* "to wander away, go astray," literally and figuratively, from *ab* "off, away from" + *errare* "to wander, stray, roam, rove"

Aliferous[U(1)]:

having wings

Etymology: from Latin, *ala* "wing" + *ferous* "bearing; producing"

Altisonant:

lofty or pompous; high language

Synonyms:	pretentious (in language)
Antonyms:	basic (in language)

Etymology: from *alti-*, Latin *altus* "high; (lit.) grown tall" + *sonant* "uttered with vocal sound," from Latin *sonantem* (nominative *sonans*), present participle of *sonare* "make a noise, sound".

Amphoric[U]:

resembling the sound made by blowing across the mouth of an empty bottle

Etymology: from Latin *amphora* from Greek *amphoreus* "an amphora, jar with two handles, urn," a contraction of *amphiphoreus*, literally "two-handled," from *amphi* "on both sides" + *phoreus* "bearer," from *pherein* "to bear", from Proto-Indo European root bher "to carry".

Anachronistic:

of an error in chronology; the state or condition of being chronologically out of place, especially of things or people belonging to an earlier time

Synonyms:	antiquated; archaic; obsolete
Antonyms:	modern; updated; current

Etymology: from Latin *anachronismus*, from Greek *anakhronismos*, from *anakhronizein* "refer to wrong time," from *ana* "against" + *khronos* "time".

Callipygian[U]:

having shapely buttocks

Etymology: Latinized from Greek *kallipygos*, from *kalli-*, of *kallos* "beauty" + *pygē*" rump, buttocks.

Copacetic:

very satisfactory.

Synonyms:	adequate; satisfying; fair
Antonyms:	intolerable; insufficient

Etymology: Origin Unknown

Contumacious:

insubordinate; rebellious; disobedient

Synonyms:	headstrong; obstinate
Antonyms:	obedient; subordinate

Etymology: from Latin *contumaci-*, stem of *contumax* "haughty, insolent, obstinate" + -ous.

Convivial:

relating to, occupied with, or fond of feasting, drinking, and good company; good company.

Synonyms:	cheerful; jovial; fun-loving
Antonyms:	boorish; dour; melancholic

Etymology: from Late Latin *convivialis* "pertaining to a feast," from Latin *convivium* "a feast," from *convivere* "to carouse together, live together," from assimilated form of *com* "with, together" + *vivere* "to live".

Effable:

capable of being uttered or expressed.

Synonyms:	speakable
Antonyms:	unspeakable; unmentionable

Etymology: from French *effable* or directly, from Latin *effabilis* "utterable," from *effari* "to utter".

Erudite:

having or showing knowledge that is gained by studying.

Synonyms:	knowledgeable; scholarly
Antonyms:	uneducated; ignorant

Etymology: from Latin *eruditus* "learned, accomplished, well-informed," past participle of *erudire* "to educate, teach, instruct, polish," literally "to bring out of the rough," from assimilated form of *ex* "out" + *rudis* "unskilled, rough, unlearned"

Fatuous:

complacently or inanely foolish.

Synonyms:	stupid; absurd; asinine; foolish
Antonyms:	aware; intelligent; wise

Etymology: from Latin *fatuus* "foolish, insipid, silly"

Filipendulous[U]:

suspended by a thread

Etymology: from Latin *filum* "thread" + *pendulus* "hanging down"

Flocculent[U]:

wooly; fluffy

Etymology: from Latin *floccus* "lock of hair, tuft of wool," + -ulent

Ignominious:

marked with or characterized by shame or disgrace.

Synonyms:	embarrassing; shameful; humiliating
Antonyms:	uplifting; respectable

Etymology: from Latin *ignominiosus* "disgraceful, shameful," from *ignominia* "disgrace, infamy, loss of a (good) name," from assimilated form of *in-* "not, opposite of" + *nomen* "name".

Indecipherable:

unable to be understood.

Synonyms:	cryptic; illegible; unintelligible
Antonyms:	understandable

Etymology: unknown origin, perhaps a loan from French *dechiffrer*, combining *in-* "not, opposite of" + *de-* "completely" + *cipher* "to write in code or occult characters" + *-able* "possible".

Ineffable:

too great or extreme to be described in words; not to be uttered

Synonyms:	transcendent; indescribable; unspeakable
Antonyms:	definable; describable

Etymology: from Old French *ineffable* or directly from Latin *ineffabilis* "unutterable," from *in-* "not, opposite of" + *effabilis* "speakable," from *effari* "utter," from assimilated form of *ex* "out" + *fari* "to say, speak".

Insouciance:

lighthearted unconcern; nonchalance

Synonyms:	indifference; insensitivity
Antonyms:	interest; concern

Etymology: from French *insouciance* "heedless indifference or unconcern," from *insouciant* "carelessness, thoughtlessness, heedlessness," from *in-* "not" + *souciant* "caring," present participle of *soucier* "to care," from Latin *sollicitare* "to agitate"

Irenic:

favoring, or conducive to, or operating toward peace, moderation, or conciliation.

Synonyms:	peaceful; amiable; amicable
Antonyms:	chaotic; unfriendly

Etymology: from Greek *eirēnikos*, from *eirēnē* "peace, time of peace," a word of unknown etymology.

Jocund:

marked by or suggestive of high spirits and lively mirthfulness

Synonyms:	cheerful; blithe; elated
Antonyms:	sad; dour; down

Etymology: from Old French *jocond* or directly from Late Latin *iocundus*, variant (influenced by *iocus* "joke") of Latin *iucundus* "pleasant, agreeable," originally "helpful," contraction of *iuvicundus*, from *iuvare* "to please, benefit, help, give strength, support".

Lithe:

(especially of a person's body) thin, supple, graceful

Synonyms:	flexible; graceful; slender
Antonyms:	clumsy; rigid; stiff

Etymology: from Old English *liðe* "soft, mild, gentle, calm, meek," also, of persons, "gracious, kind, agreeable," from Proto-Germanic *linthja-*.

Lugubrious:

exaggeratedly or affectedly mournful; gloomy

Synonyms:	mournful; sorrowful; dismal
Antonyms:	happy; cheerful; excited

Etymology: from *lugere* "to mourn," from Proto-Indo European root *leug-* "to break; to cause pain".

Madid:

wet, moist

Synonyms:	dank; wet; moist
Antonyms:	dry; arid

Etymology: from Latin *madeo* "moist, wet", from Proto-Indo European root *mehd* "to drip, ooze".

Mellifluous:

having a smooth, rich flow (e.g. honey, a voice); filled with something that sweetens.

Synonyms:	smooth; sweet-sounding
Antonyms:	discordant; cacophonous; rocky

Etymology: from Late Latin *mellifluus* "flowing with (or as if with) honey," from Latin *mel* (genitive *mellis*) "honey" (related to Greek *meli* "honey;" from Proto-Indo European root *melit-* "honey") + *-fluus* "flowing," from *fluere* "to flow".

Noctivagant[U]:

going about in the night; night wandering

Etymology: from Latin *noct-*, stem of *nox* "night" + *vagantem* (nominative *vagans*), present participle of *vagari* "to wander, stroll about, roam, be unsettled, spread abroad," from *vagus* "roving, wandering".

Obdurate:

to be stubborn in wrongdoing.

Synonyms:	stubborn
Antonyms:	amenable; abiding

Etymology: from Latin *obduratus* "hardened," past participle of *obdurare* "harden, render hard; be hard or hardened; hold out, persist, endure," from *ob* "against" + *durare* "harden, render hard," from *durus* "hard," from Proto-Indo European *dru-ro-*, suffixed variant form of root *deru-*"be firm, solid, steadfast."

Obstreperous:

marked by unruly or aggressive noisiness; stubbornly resistant to control

Synonyms:	noisy; unruly; clamorous
Antonyms:	quiet; submissive; demure

Etymology: from Latin *obstreperus* "clamorous," from *obstrepere* "drown with noise, make a noise against, oppose noisily," from *ob* "against" + *strepere* "make a noise".

Parsimonious:

frugal to the point of stinginess.

Synonyms:	stingy; penny-pinching
Antonyms:	giving; charitableness

Etymology: from Latin *parsimonia* "frugality, thrift" + -ous, where from *pars-* is the past-participle stem of *parcere* "to spare, save, refrain from, use moderately" + -*monia*, suffix signifying action, state, or condition.

Perfidious:

deceitful and untrustworthy.

Synonyms:	treacherous; scheming
Antonyms:	trustworthy; honest

Etymology: from Latin *perfidiosus* "treacherous," from *perfidia* "faithlessness", where from *perfidus* means "faithless," from phrase *per fidem decipere* "to deceive through trustingness," from *per* "through" + *fidem* (nominative *fides*) "faith".

Perspicacious:

of acute mental vision or discernment

Synonyms:	acute; alert; astute
Antonyms:	ignorant; unaware; unobservant

Etymology: formed as an adjective to perspicacity, from Latin *perspicax* "sharp-sighted, having the power of seeing through; acute," from *perspicere* "look through, look closely at," from *per* "through", from Proto-Indo European root *per-* "forward," hence "through" + *specere* "look at", from Proto-Indo European root *spek-* "to observe".

Prionodont[U]:

having a sawlike row of simple and similar teeth.

Etymology: from *prion-,* from Greek *priōn* "a saw," + *-odont* "teeth, toothed", from Ancient Greek ὀδούς (*odoús*).

Putative:

commonly accepted or supposed.

Synonyms:	presumed; reputed
Antonyms:	

Etymology: from Late Latin *putativus* "supposed," from *putat-*, past-participle stem of Latin *putare* "to judge, suppose, believe, suspect," originally "to clean, trim, prune", from Proto-Indo European root *pau-* "to cut, strike, stamp".

Quiescent:

marked by inactivity or repose; tranquility at rest

Synonyms:	inactive; tranquil
Antonyms:	active; frantic

Etymology: from Latin *quiescentem* (nominative *quiescens*), present participle of *quiescere*, inchoative verb formed from *quies* "rest, quiet", from suffixed form of Proto-Indo European root *kweie-* "to rest, be quiet".

Quixotic:

extremely idealistic; unpractical, unrealistic

Synonyms:	foolish; impractical; impulsive
Antonyms:	grounded; realistic

Etymology: from Don *Quixote.*

Rapacious:

excessively grasping or covetous.

Synonyms:	greedy;
Antonyms:	giving; charitable; satisfied

Etymology: from Latin *rapaci-*, stem of *rapax* "grasping," itself from stem of *rapere* "to seize" + -ous.

Sagacious:

of keen and farsighted judgment; wise, discerning

Synonyms:	judicious; astute
Antonyms:	unaware; careless; foolish

Etymology: from French *sagacité*, from Latin *sagacitatem* (nominative *sagacitas*) "keenness of perception, quality of being acute," from *sagax* "of quick perception, acute," related to *sagus* "prophetic," *sagire* "perceive keenly", from Proto-Indo European root *sag-* "to track down, trace, seek".

Salubrious:

health-giving, favorable to bringing health; healthy

Synonyms:	beneficial; healthy
Antonyms:	unhealthy; damaging

Etymology: from Latin *salubris* "promoting health, healthful," from *salus* (genitive *salutis*) "welfare, health", from Proto-Indo European root *sol-* "whole, well-kept".

Sanguine:

confident and hopeful

Synonyms:	buoyant; optimistic; cheerful
Antonyms:	pessimistic; insecure

Etymology: from Old French *sanguin* (fem. *sanguine*) and directly from Latin *sanguineus* "of blood," also "bloody, bloodthirsty," from *sanguis* (genitive *sanguinis*) "blood".

Obscure Fact: The meaning "cheerful, hopeful, vivacious, confident" is attested by C.E. 1500, because these qualities were thought in old medicine to spring from an excess or predominance of blood as one of the four humors. The sense of "of or pertaining to blood" is rare.

Saturnine:

cold and steady in mood; of gloomy or surly disposition

Synonyms:	depressed; cheerless
Antonyms:	joyous; jocose

Etymology: from Middle English *Saturne* + -ine.

Obscure Fact: Old medicine believed these characteristics to be caused or influenced by the astrological influence of the planet Saturn, which was the most remote from the Sun (in the knowledge of the times) and thus coldest and slowest in its revolution.

Scripturient[U]:

having a strong urge to write.

Etymology: late Latin *scripturient-, scripturiens*, present participle of *scripturire* to desire to write, desiderative of Latin *scribere*.

Selcouth:

unusual, strange

Synonyms:	different; unusual
Antonyms:	normal; average

Etymology: Middle English, from Old English *seldcūth*, from *seldan* seldom + *cūth* known.

Sibilant[U]:

having, containing, or producing a hissing
or *sh* or *s* sound.

Etymology: from Latin *sibilantem* (nominative *sibilans*),
present participle of *sibilare* "to hiss, whistle".

Splenetic:

marked by a bad temper, malevolence, or spite.

Synonyms:	acrimonious; bitter; caustic; petulant
Antonyms:	happy; helping; kind

Etymology: from Late Latin *spleneticus*, from *splen*.

Spurious:

not being what it purports to be; false, fake

Synonyms:	counterfeit; fake; untrue
Antonyms:	true; real; authentic

Etymology: from Latin *spurius* "illegitimate, false", from *spurius* (n.) "illegitimate child," probably from Etruscan *spural* "public."

Supernal:

relating to the sky or heavens; celestial

Synonyms:	ethereal
Antonyms:	

Etymology: from Old French *supernal* "supreme" and directly from Medieval Latin *supernalis*, from Latin *supernus* "situated above, that is above; celestial", from *super* "above, over;" from Proto-Indo European root *uper "over".

Telic[U]:

trending toward an end or outcome;
purposeful

Etymology: from Latinized form of Greek *telikos* "final,"
from *telos* "end, goal, result".

Temerous:

rash, reckless

Synonyms:	audacious; nerve; careless
Antonyms:	cautionious; careful; tempered

Etymology: from Latin *temere* "indiscreetly, rashly, by chance".

Tendentious:

biased

Synonyms:	prejudicial; unfair
Antonyms:	unbiased; fair;

Etymology: from or modeled on German *tendenziös*, from *Tendenz* "tendency," from Medieval Latin *tendentia* "inclination, leaning," from Latin *tendens*, present participle of *tendere* "to stretch, extend, aim".

Tenebrous:

shut off from light; dark, gloomy

Synonyms:	dark; ominous;
Antonyms:	lightful; inviting

Etymology: from Old French *tenebros* "dark, gloomy", from Latin *tenebrosus* "dark," from *tenebrae* "darkness," from Proto-Indo European root *temsro-* "dark" (adj.).

Turbid:

thick or opaque as if roiled by sediment; heavy with smoke or mist; characterized by or producing obscurity (as of mind or emotions)

Synonyms:	cloudy; impaired
Antonyms:	clear

Etymology: from Latin *turbidus* "muddy, full of confusion," from *turbare* "to confuse, bewilder," from *turba* "turmoil, crowd".

Turgid:

excessively embellished in style or language; being in a state of distention

Synonyms:	swollen; embellished
Antonyms:	humble; modest

Etymology: from Latin *turgidus* "swollen, inflated, distended," from *turgere* "to swell," of unknown origin.

Umbral:

Shaded

Synonyms:	shadowy; dark; shady
Antonyms:	bright; lighted

Etymology: from Latin *umbra* "shade, shadow".

Vespertine[U]:

of or relating to twilight, evening.

Etymology: from Latin *vespertinus* "of the evening," from *vesper* "evening".

Verdant:

abundant in plants and flowers; green

Synonyms:	lush; blooming; green
Antonyms:	decaying

Etymology: from French *virdeant* "becoming green," present participle of Old French *verdeiier* "become green," from Vulgar Latin *viridiare* "grow green, make green," from Latin *viridis* "green".

Virid[U]:

vividly green; verdant.

Etymology: from Latin *virid-*, stem of *viridis* "green, blooming, vigorous".

Vitreous:

of, having the nature of, or like, glass

Synonyms:	glassy
Antonyms:	

Etymology: from Latin *vitreus* "of glass, glassy," from *vitrum* "glass".

Voluble:

characterized by a ready and continuous flow of words

Synonyms:	loquacious; talkative
Antonyms:	quiet; silent

Etymology: from Latin *volubilis* "that turns around, rolling, flowing," figuratively (of speech) "fluent, rapid," from *volvere* "to turn around, roll", from Proto-Indo European root *wel-* (3) "to turn, revolve".

Vulpine[U]:

of, relating to, or resembling a fox

Etymology: from Latin *vulpinus* "of or pertaining to a fox," from *vulpes*, earlier *volpes* "fox," from Proto-Indo European *wlpe-* "fox".

Xanthous[U]:

having yellowish, red, auburn, or brown hair; marked by a yellow coloration

Etymology: from Greek *xanthos* "yellow," of unknown origin.

Nouns

Acumen:

keenness and depth of perception, discernment, or discrimination especially in practical matters.

Synonyms:	awareness; insight; discernment; acuity
Antonyms:	ignorance; stupidity

Etymology: from Latin *acumen* "a point, sting," hence, figuratively, "mental sharpness, shrewdness," from *acuere* "to sharpen," literal and figurative (of intellect, emotion, etc.), related to *acus* "a needle", from PIE root *ak-* "be sharp, rise (out) to a point, pierce".

Agelast[U]:

a person who never laughs.

Etymology: borrowed from Middle French *agelaste*, borrowed from Greek *agélastos* "not laughing, grave, gloomy," from *a-* + *gelastós*, verbal adjective of *gelân* "to laugh".

Ambsace[U]:

the lowest throw at dice; something worthless or unlucky

Etymology: from Middle English *ambes as*, from Anglo-French, from *ambes* "both" + *as* "aces".

Anathema:

a person or thing detested or loathed.

Synonyms:	bane; pariah
Antonyms:	(something) loved

Etymology: from Latin *anathema* "an excommunicated person; the curse of excommunication," from Ecclesiastical Greek *anathema* "a thing accursed," a slight variation of classical Greek *anathama*, which meant merely "a thing devoted," literally "a thing set up (to the gods)," such as a votive offering in a temple, from *ana* "up" + *tithenai* "to put, to place", from reduplicated form of Proto-Indo European root *dhe-* "to set, put".

Anomie[U]:

social instability resulting from a breakdown of standards or values in a society; personal unrest, alienation, and uncertainty that comes from a lack of purpose or ideals

Etymology: a reborrowing with French spelling of *anomy*, from Greek *anomia* "lawlessness," abstract noun from *anomos* "without law, lawless," from *a-* "without" + *nomos* "law".

Antidisestablishmentarianism[U]:

opposition to the belief that there should not be an official relationship between a country's government and its national Church

Etymology: the establishment is "the ecclesiastical system established by law" (1731), specifically "the Church of England" (1731). Hence *establishmentarianism* "the principle of a state church" (1846) and *disestablishment* "act of withdrawing (a church) from a privileged relation to the state", which are married in this word.

Obscure Fact: This word is rarely used in modern vocabulary, and is most often encountered in lists of the longest English words!

Antiquitarian[U]:

one who is attached to the opinions or practices of antiquity.

Etymology: from Latin *antiquarius* "pertaining to antiquity," from *antiquuus* "ancient, aged, venerable".

Apricity[U]:

the warmth of the sun in winter.

Etymology: *Apricity* appears to have entered our language in 1623, when Henry Cockeram recorded (or possibly invented) it for his dictionary *The English Dictionary; or, An Interpreter of Hard English Words.*

Obscure Fact: This word never really caught on despite its beautiful meaning, and will not be found in any modern dictionary aside from the *Oxford English Dictionary.*

Apocatastasis[U]:

restitution, restoration; specifically the final restoration of all sinful beings to God and to the state of blessedness.

Etymology: derived from the Greek verb *apokathistemi*, which means "to restore".

Obscure Fact: This first emerged as a doctrine in Zoroastrianism, where it represents the end of history for the religion, when evil is destroyed and the world is restored to an original state of goodness.

Ataraxia:

calmness untroubled by mental or emotional disquiet

Synonyms:	calm; content; relaxation
Antonyms:	agitation; discontent; unhappiness

Etymology: from Modern Latin, from Greek *ataraxia* "impassiveness," from *a-* "not, without" + *tarassein* "to disturb, confuse", from Proto-Indo European root *dhrehgh-* "to confuse".

Clowder[U]:

a group of cats.

Etymology: A variation, recorded since 1801, of *clutter*, itself from *clot*, from Old English *clott* ("round mass, lump"), from Proto-Germanic *klūtaz*.

Consternation:

a sudden, alarming amazement or dread that results in utter confusion; dismay; fear resulting from the awareness of danger.

Synonyms:	terror; bewilderment; panic
Antonyms:	calm; assurance; contentment

Etymology: from French *consternation* "dismay, confusion," from Latin *consternationem* (nominative *consternatio*) "confusion, dismay," noun of state from past-participle stem of *consternare* "overcome, confuse, dismay, perplex, terrify, alarm," which is probably related to *consternere* "throw down, prostrate," from assimilated form of *com-* + *sternere* "to spread out, lay down, stretch out", from nasalized form of Proto-Indo European root *stere-* "to spread".

Creche[U]:

a Nativity scene.

Etymology: from French *crèche*, from Old French *cresche*, *creche* "crib, manger, stall" (13c.), ultimately from Frankish or some other Germanic source.

Cryalgesia[U]:

pain due to cold

Etymology: from *cryo-,* from Ancient Greek *krúos* "icy cold; chill, frost" + *álgēsis*, "sense of pain".

Cryptonym[U]:

a secret name

Etymology: from *crypto-* "secret, hidden" + *-onym* "name," from Greek, from Proto-Indo European root *nomen-* "name".

Cupidity:

inordinate desire for wealth; avarice, greed

Synonyms:	avarice; greed; longing
Antonyms:	apathy; generosity; charitableness

Etymology: from Anglo-French *cupidite* and directly from Latin *cupiditatem* (nominative *cupiditas*) "passionate desire, lust; ambition," from *cupidus* "eager, passionate," from *cupere* "to desire." Perhaps from a Proto-Indo European root *kup-(e)i-* "to tremble; to desire".

Ebullience:

the quality of lively or enthusiastic expression of thoughts or feelings.

Synonyms:	exuberance; enthusiasm
Antonyms:	indifference; sadness; depression

Etymology: from Latin *ebullientem* (nominative *ebulliens*) "a boiling, a bursting forth, overflow," present participle of *ebullire* "to boil over".

Episteme[U]:

knowledge, specifically intellectually certain knowledge.

Etymology: from Greek *episteme* "knowledge".

Eunoia[U]:

a feeling of goodwill

Etymology: from Greek *eus* "good," *eu* "well" + *-noia* "mind", where from Proto-Indo European *(e)su-* "good", originally a suffixed form of root *es-* "to be."

Eventide:

the time of evening.

Synonyms:	dusk; evening; nightfall
Antonyms:	morning; daytime

Etymology: Old English *æfentid* "evening".

Flinders[U]:

small fragments or splinters

Etymology: Scottish *flendris*, probably related to Norwegian *flindra* "chip, splinter," or Dutch *flenter* "fragment;" ultimately from Proto-Germanic *flintaz*, formerly said to be from a Proto-Indo European root *(s)plei-* "to splice, split".

Floccinaucinihilipilification:

the estimation of something as valueless.

Etymology: a combination of four Latin words (*flocci, nauci, nihili, pili*) all signifying "at a small price" or "for nothing," + Latin-derived suffix *-fication* "making, causing."

Frisson[U]:

a brief moment of emotional excitement.

Etymology: from French *frisson* "fever, illness; shiver, thrill" (12c.), from Latin *frigere* "to be cold", related to noun *frigus* "cold, coldness, frost," from Proto-Italic *srigos-*, from Proto-Indo European root *srig-* "cold".

Gloaming[U]:

twilight, dusk

Etymology: Old English *glomung* "twilight, the fall of evening," from *glom* "twilight," which is related to *glowan* "to glow", from Proto-Germanic *glo-* "glow".

Griffonage[U]:

careless handwriting; crude or illegible scrawl

Etymology: from French, *griffonner* "to scribble, scrawl" from *griffer* "to scratch" (from Old French *grifer*, either from *griffe* "to scratch", or from Old High German *grīfan* "to gripe", from Proto-Germanic *grīpaną* "to grab, grasp") + *-onner*.

Lacuna:

a gap.

Synonyms:	pause; break; hiatus
Antonyms:	continuity; closure

Etymology: from Latin *lacuna* "hole, pit," figuratively "a gap, void, want," diminutive of *lacus* "pond, lake; hollow, opening".

Lethologica[U]:

the inability to remember a particular word or name

Etymology: from Ancient Greek *léthē*, "forgetfulness" + *lógos*, "word".

Locution:

a style of discourse; a peculiarity of phrasing.

Synonyms:	inflection
Antonyms:	

Etymology: from Latin *locutionem* (nominative *locutio*) "a speaking, speech, discourse; way of speaking," noun of action from past-participle stem of *loqui* "to speak," from Proto-Indo European root *tolkw-* "to speak."

Melange:

a medley or mixture

Synonyms:	jumble; medly
Antonyms:	

Etymology: from French *mélange* (15c.), from *mêler* "to mix, mingle," from Old French *mesler* to mix, meddle, mingle", from Vulgar Latin **misculare*, from Latin *miscere* "to mix" from Proto-Indo European root *meik-* "to mix".

Metanoia[U]:

a transformative change of heart.

Etymology: from Greek *metanoia* "afterthought, repentance," from *metanoein* "to change one's mind or purpose," from *meta,* here indicating "change" + *noein* "to have mental perception," from *noos* "mind, thought," which is of uncertain origin.

Myrmidon:

a follower or subordinate of a powerful person, typically one who is unscrupulous or carries out orders unquestioningly.

Synonyms:	comrade; disciple; follower; cohort
Antonyms:	enemy; foe

Etymology: from Latin *Myrmidones* (plural), from Greek *Myrmidones*, Thessalian tribe led by Achilles to the Trojan War, fabled to have been ants changed into men, and often derived from Greek *myrmex* "ant", from PIE *morwi-* "ant".

Munificence:

the quality or state of being very generous.

Synonyms:	generosity; benevolence
Antonyms:	malevolence; miserly

Etymology: from Old French *munificence*, from Latin *munificentia* "bountifulness, liberality, generosity," from stem of *munificus* "generous, bountiful, liberal," literally "present-making," from *munus* "gift or service; function, task, duty, office" + unstressed stem of *facere* "to do" from Proto-Indo European root *dhe-* "to set, put".

Oneiromancy[U]:

the interpretation of dreams to predict or foretell the future

Etymology: from Greek *oneiros* "a dream," a word of uncertain origin + Old French *-mancie*, from Late Latin *-mantia*, from Greek *manteia* "oracle, divination," from *mantis* "one who divines, a seer, prophet; one touched by divine madness," from *mainesthai* "be inspired," which is related to *menos* "passion, spirit", from Proto-Indo European *mnyo-*, suffixed form of root men- "to think".

Orrery[U]:

an apparatus showing the relative positions
and motions of bodies in the solar system
by balls moved by a clockwork

Etymology: invented c. 1704 by English clockmaker
George Graham (1673-1751) and constructed by
instrument maker John Rowley. Graham gave a copy to
his patron, Charles Boyle (1674-1731), 4th Earl of *Orrery*
(Cork) and named it in his honor.

Overmorrow[U]:

the day after tomorrow.

Etymology: from *over,* Old English *ofer* "beyond; above, in place or position higher than; upon; in; across, past; more than; on high," from Proto-Germanic *uberi,* from PIE root *uper* "over." + *morrow,* from Old English *to morgenne* "on (the) morrow," from *morgenne,* dative of *morgen* "morning".

Panacea[U]:

a cure all.

Etymology: from Latin *panacea*, a herb (variously identified) that would heal all illnesses, from Greek *panakeia* "cure-all," from *panakēs* "all-healing," from *pan-* "all" + *akos* "cure," from *iasthai* "to heal".

Paucity[U]:

a lack of something; scarcity

Synonyms:	dearth; insufficiency
Antonyms:	abundance; plentifulness

Etymology: from Old French *paucité* and directly from Latin *paucitatem* (nominative *paucitas*) "fewness, scarcity, a small number," from *paucus* "few, little," from Proto-Indo European *pau-ko-*, suffixed form of root *pau-* (1) "few, little".

Penumbra[U]:

a space of partial illumination (as in an eclipse) between the perfect shadow on all sides and the full light

Etymology: from Modern Latin *penumbra* "partial shadow outside the complete shadow of an eclipse," coined 1604 by Kepler from Latin *pæne* "nearly, almost, practically," which is of uncertain origin, + *umbra* "shadow".

Perdition:

eternal damnation or punishment

Synonyms:	hell; damnation; punishment
Antonyms:	exoneration; redemption; bliss

Etymology: from Old French *perdicion* "loss, calamity, perdition" of souls and directly from Late Latin *perditionem* "ruin, destruction," noun of action from past-participle stem of Latin *perdere* "do away with, destroy; lose, throw away, squander," from *per-* "through" (here perhaps with intensive or completive force, "to destruction") + *dare* "to give", from Proto-Indo European root *do-* "to give".

Persiflage[U]:

frivolous bantering talk; light mockery

Etymology: from French *persiflage*, from *persifler* "to banter", from Latin *per* "through", from PIE root per- "forward," hence "through" + French *siffler* "to whistle, hiss," from collateral form of Latin *sibilare* "to hiss".

Petrichor[U]:

a distinct, earthy, usually pleasant odor
associated with the rain.

Etymology: constructed from Ancient Greek *pétra*
"rock", or *pétros* "stone", and *ikhṓr*, the ethereal fluid that
is the blood of the gods in Greek mythology.

Prig:

a self-righteously moralistic person who behaves as if they were superior to other people.

Synonyms:	moralizer
Antonyms:	

Etymology: Unknown Origin.

Raconteur[U]:

a person who excels in storytelling.

Etymology: from French *raconteur*, from *raconter* "to recount, tell, narrate," from *re-* + Old French *aconter* "to count, render account".

Reverie:

daydream; to be lost in your own thoughts.

Synonyms:	daydream; contemplation; trance
Antonyms:	

Etymology: from Old French *reverie*, *resverie* "revelry, rejoicing, wantonness, raving, delirium", a word of uncertain origin.

Serendipity:

a string of chance events that leads to a happy outcome.

Synonyms:	fortunate; happenstance
Antonyms:	misfortune

Etymology: coined by Horace Walpole in a letter to Horace Mann that is dated Jan. 28, 1754.

Snuggery:

a small, cozy place

Synonyms:	den; nest
Antonyms:	

Etymology: Unknown Origin.

Solivagant[U]:

a solitary wanderer

Etymology: from Latin *solivag*us wandering alone (from *soli-* + *vagus* wandering) + *-ant*.

Sobriquet:

a descriptive name or epithet; a person's nickname

Synonyms:	nickname
Antonyms:	

Etymology: from French *sobriquet* "nickname," from French *soubriquet*, which also meant "a jest, quip,"

Sonder[U]:

"the realization that each random passerby is living a life as vivid and complex as your own—populated with their own ambitions, friends, routines, worries and inherited craziness—an epic story that continues invisibly around you like an anthill sprawling deep underground, with elaborate passageways to thousands of other lives that you'll never know existed, in which you might appear only once, as an extra sipping coffee in the background, as a blur of traffic passing on the highway, as a lighted window at dusk."

Etymology: Coined by U.S. Author John Koenig for his blog, *The Dictionary of Obscure Sorrows.*[3]

Specie[U]:

money in the form of coins rather than notes.

Etymology: from the Medieval Latin phrase *in specie* "in minted coins".

Stardust[U]:

a feeling or impression of romance, magic, or ethereality

Etymology: Unknown Origin.

Susurrus:

a whispering or rustling sound

Synonyms:	whisper; rustling; murmur
Antonyms:	scream; shriek

Etymology: from Latin *susurrationem*, noun of action from past-participle stem of *susurrare* "to hum, murmur," from *susurrus* "a murmur, whisper." This is held to be a reduplication of a PIE imitative *swer-* "to buzz, whisper".

Sybarite[U]:

a person who is self indulgent in their fondness for sensuous luxury.

Etymology: literally "inhabitant of *Sybaris*," ancient Greek town in southern Italy (720-510 B.C.E.), whose people were noted for their love of luxury. From Latin *Sybarita*, from Greek *Sybaritēs*.

Synastry[U]:

concurrence of starry position or influence upon two persons : similarity of condition or fortune prefigured by astrology

Etymology: from Late Latin *synastria*, from Greek, from *syn-* "acting or considered together" + *astr-* "star" + *-ia* -y.

Syzygy[U]:

the nearly straight line of three celestial bodies in a solar system aligning

Etymology: from Late Latin *syzygia*, from Greek *syzygia* "yoke of animals, pair, union of two, conjunction," from *syzygein* "to yoke together," from assimilated form of *syn-* "together" + *zygon* "yoke", from Proto-Indo European root *yeug-* "to join".

Tergiversation:

evasion of straightforward action or a clear cut statement; desertion of a cause, position, party, or faith.

Synonyms:	defection; deflection
Antonyms:	loyalty; honesty

Etymology: from Latin *tergiversationem* (nominative *tergiversatio*) "a shifting, evasion, declining, refusing," noun of action from past-participle stem of *tergiversari*. This is, etymologically, "to turn one's back on," thus "evade," from *tergum* "the back" (a word of unknown origin) + *versare* "to spin, turn," frequentative of *vertere* "to turn", from Proto-Indo European root *wer-* "to turn, bend".

Thanatophobia[U]:

the extreme or unusual fear of death.

Etymology: from *thanat-*, word-forming element meaning "death," from Greek *thanatos* "death," from Proto-Indo European *dhwene-* "to disappear, die" + *-phobia* "intense fear".

Ultracrepidarian[U]:

someone who has no special knowledge of a subject but who expresses an opinion on it.

Etymology: from Latin *ultrā crepidam* (also *suprā crepidam*) "above the sole, beyond the sole," from adverb and preposition *ultrā* + Latin *crepidam* (accusative singular of *crepida*) "sole of a shoe, shoe, sandal" (re-formed from Greek *krēpîd-,* stem of *krēpís* "man's high boot, half boot, shoe") + -arian.

Uxoricide[U]:

the murder of a wife by her husband.

Etymology: from French *uxoricide,* or else a native
formation from Latin *uxor* "wife" + *-cide* "killing/killer."

Victual[U]:

food or provisions

Etymology: from Anglo-French and Old French *vitaille* "food, nourishment, provisions," from Late Latin *victualia* "provisions," noun use of plural of *victualis* "of nourishment," from *victus* "livelihood, food, sustenance, that which sustains life," from past participle stem of *vivere* "to live", from Proto-Indo European root *gwei-* "to live".

Viduity[U]:

widowhood.

Etymology: from Middle English (Scots) *viduite*, from Middle French *viduité*, from Latin *viduitat-*, *viduitas*, from *vidua* "widow" + *-itat-*, *-itas -ity*.

Zephyr[U]:

a very slight or gentle wind.

Etymology: from Latin *Zephyrus*, from Greek *Zephyros* "the west wind".

Zymurgy[U]:

the study or practice of fermentation for brewing beer, wine, or distilled spirits.

Etymology: from Greek *zymo-*, combining form of *zymē* "a leaven", from Proto-Indo European root **yeue-* +
-ourgia "a working," from *ergon* "work", from Proto-Indo European root *werg-* "to do".

Verbs

Abscond:

to leave in a fast and secretive manner, often to avoid arrest or prosecution.

Synonyms:	to run away
Antonyms:	

Etymology: from French *abscondre* "to hide" and directly from Latin *abscondere* "to hide, conceal, put out of sight," from assimilated form of *ab* "off, away from" + *condere* "put together, store," from assimilated form of *com-* "together" + *-dere* "put", from Proto-Indo European root *dhe-* "to put, place".

Ameliorate:

to mend, to make better.

Synonyms:	to alleviate; to mitigate
Antonyms:	aggravate; inflame; worsen

Etymology: from Medieval Latin *amelioratus*, past participle of *ameliorare*.

Apricate[U]:

to bask in the sunshine.

Etymology: from Latin *apricatus*, past participle of *apricari* "to bask in the sun," from *apricus* "exposed" (to the sun; the antonym of *opacus* "shady").

Balter[U]:

to dance or tread clumsily or without skill.

Etymology: from Middle English *balteren*.

Carouse:

to drink liquor freely and excessively

Synonyms:	to revel
Antonyms:	to sober (up)

Etymology: from French *carousser* "drink, quaff, swill," from German *gar aus* "quite out," from *gar austrinken*; *trink garaus* "to drink up entirely.

Coruscate[U]:

to flash, to sparkle, to glitter.

Synonyms:	gleam; glisten
Antonyms:	

Etymology: from Latin *coruscatus*, past participle of *coruscare* "to vibrate, glitter".

Defenestrate[U]:

to throw somebody out of a window

Etymology: from Latin *fenestra* "window."

Obscure Fact: this word was invented for one incident: the "Defenestration of Prague," May 21, 1618, when two Catholic deputies to the Bohemian national assembly and a secretary were tossed out the window of the castle of Hradschin by Protestant radicals (the pair landed in a trash heap and survived). It marked the start of the Thirty Years' War.

Emblaze:

to make more attractive by adding something that is beautiful or becoming; to illuminate with flame

Synonyms:	adorn; gild; decorate
Antonyms:	

Etymology: from Old French *blason* "a shield, blazon," also "collar bone;" a common Romanic word but one of uncertain origin.

Fenestrate[U]:

to furnish with windows or openings

Etymology: from Latin *fenestra* "window."

Gyve[U]:

to shackle, chain

Etymology: from Middle English *give*, *gyve* "to shackle; shackles".

Hebetate[U]:

to make dull or obtuse

Etymology: from Latin *hebetatus*, past participle of *hebetare*, from *hebes* "dull, blunt".

Harangue[U]:

to speak to someone or a group of people, often for a long time, in a forceful and often angry way, usually in an attempt to persuade them

Etymology: from French *harangue* "a public address", from Old Italian *aringo* "public square, platform; pulpit; arena," from a Germanic source such as Old High German *hring* "circle".

Maunder:

to talk in a rambling way; to move or act in a dreamy or idle manner.

Synonyms:	to digress; to ramble
Antonyms:	

Etymology: from frequentative of *maund* "to beg", which is possibly from French *mendier* "to beg," from Latin *mendicare* "to beg, ask alms".

Mendicate[U]:

to beg

Etymology: from Latin *mendicantem* (nominative *mendicans*) present participle of *mendicare* "to beg, ask alms," from *mendicus* "beggar," originally "cripple", from *menda* "fault, physical defect," from Proto-Indo European root *mend-* "physical defect, fault".

Occlude:

to block off.

Synonyms:	to prevent; to block; to close-off
Antonyms:	to open; to facilitate

Etymology: from Latin *occludere* "shut up, close up," from assimilated form of *ob* "in front of, against" + *claudere* "to shut, close".

Obfuscate:

to throw into shadow; to darken; to create unsurity.

Synonyms:	to confuse; to hide (something)
Antonyms:	to clear; to elucidate

Etymology: from Latin *obfuscatus*, past participle of *obfuscare* "to darken" (usually in a figurative sense), from *ob* "in front of, before" + *fuscare* "to make dark," from *fuscus* "dark".

Peregrinate:

to travel, especially on foot; to walk

Synonyms:	to journey
Antonyms:	to remain

Etymology: from Latin *peregrinatus*, past participle of *peregrinari* "to travel abroad, be alien," figuratively "to wander, roam, travel about," from *peregrinus* "from foreign parts, foreigner," from *peregre* "abroad," properly "from abroad, found outside Roman territory," from *per* "away" + *agri*, locative of *ager* "field, territory, land, country", from Proto-Indo European root *agro-* "field".

Prevaricate:

to lie; to deviate from the truth.

Synonyms:	to deceive; to falsify
Antonyms:	to be honest

Etymology: from Latin *praevaricatus*, past participle of *praevaricari* "to make a sham accusation, deviate" (from the path of duty), literally "walk crookedly".

Quaff:

to drink (a usually alcoholic beverage) heartily or copiously

Synonyms:	guzzle; imbibe; gulp
Antonyms:	eject; vomit

Etymology: Unknown Origin.

Revictual[U]:

to supply with provisions

Etymology: from Anglo-French and Old French *vitaille* "food, nourishment, provisions," from Late Latin *victualia* "provisions," noun use of plural of *victualis* "of nourishment," from *victus* "livelihood, food, sustenance, that which sustains life," from past participle stem of *vivere* "to live", from Proto-Indo European root *gwei-* "to live".

Reticulate:

to divide and form as a network.

Synonyms:	to associate; to mesh; to create a network
Antonyms:	to disassociate; to divide

Etymology: from Latin *reticulatus* "having a net-like pattern," from *reticulum* "little net," a double diminutive of *rete* "net," a word of uncertain origin.

Sough[U]:

(of the wind in trees, the sea, etc.) to make a moaning, whistling, or rushing sound

Etymology: Middle English *swouen,* from Old English *swogan* "to sound, roar, howl, rustle, whistle," from Proto-Germanic *swoganan* (source also of Old Saxon *swogan* "to rustle," Gothic *gaswogjan* "to sigh"), from Proto-Indo European imitative root *(s)wagh.*

Stellify[U]:

to turn into or as if to turn into a star.

Etymology: from Middle English *stellifien*, from Middle French *stellifier*, from Medieval Latin *stellificare*, from Latin *stella* star + *-ificare* -ify

Vituperate:

to blame or insult someone in strong or violent language.

Synonyms:	to abuse (by way of language)
Antonyms:	to compliment

Etymology: from Latin *vituperatus*, past participle of *vituperare*.

Suggested Words

Mirasola:

(n.) a strange feeling brought about when the sunlight in Autumn and Spring appears different or etheric

---

Etymology: from Latin, *mira* "wonders" + *solis* "of the sun".

How I made this: Think of an emotion you feel in niche and obscure circumstances. For me, this was the sunlight in Autumn, when it feels paler and ghostly and makes me feel almost nostalgic.

From there, pick a few words that summarize that emotion. For "Mirasola", the words I chose were "wonderous" and "sun". Translate these words into a root language of English (think: old German, Latin, old Norse). In this case, I translated the words into Latin. I chose the phrase "wonders of the sun", which literally looks like: *miracula solis*. Trim, conjunct, and shape.

Miracula becomes *mira* and *solis* becomes *sola*, thus we have *mirasola*!

Perinter:

(v.) to find something of value on the ground

Etymology: from Latin, *reperio* "I find" + *in* + *terra* "earth, ground".

How I made this: Think of an action you do that might be too specific for a word, currently. In this instance, finding something like a 100 dollar bill on the ground.

Again, pick a few words. Here, it is "I find" and "ground", for "I found on the ground". Translate it into a root language, to get *reper* + *io* for "I find" (*reper* being "found"), and *terra* for "ground, earth". The *in* comes from the concept of "upon". So we have *reperio* (I find) + *in* (upon) + *terra* (the ground). Altogether it could look like *repariointerra*. Shave it down to some roots, where *reperio* = *per* and *terra* = *ter*, with *in* remaining the same. Combine for *perinter*!

Suhockital:

(adj.) the state of being too intoxicated (on substances) to be comfortable, but not enough to overdose

Etymology: from German, *zu* "too" + *hock* "high", + *-ital* from Latin, *vitalus* "vital, alive".

How I made this: Think of a physical sensation you might feel at niche times. Here, it is the concept of being a little too high, but not enough to die.

Take your words – here they are *too, high, alive* – and start translating into your languages of choice. Don't be afraid to mix root languages. Here, we have *zu* from German, meaning "too" + *hock* meaning "high" + *vitalis* meaning "vital/alive". This one is pretty straightforward, in regards to the translation. "Too high, but alive."

Change *zu* to *su* to make it easier for English speakers. *Hock* can remain. Shift *vitalis* to *vital* to *-ital* to create a suffix. Combine for *suhockital*!

Vitaenodum:

(n.) the sense that one's life is too complicated for them to balance it properly

---

Etymology: from Latin, *vitae* "of life" + *nodum* "knot".

How I made this: I took inspiration from the Dictionary of Obscure Sorrows, and made an Obscure Sorrow myself! Again, think of a niche emotion. Here it is the sense that life is too complicated to balance.

Words: *life, knot*, as in "my life is in a knot". See how these words are made from basic concepts. Translate, here, in Latin: *vitae* "of life" + *nodum* "knot". Some, like this word, you can simply combine. *Vitae + nodum = vitaenodum*, the sense that one's life is in knots!

Part Two:
Grammar

Obscure Grammar and Grammatical Rules

Compound Possession

Compound Possession is easily the least obscure grammatical rule in this dictionary. You use it every day, whether you mean to or not. The central rule of Compound Possession is: if you have two people who own one thing, add the ('s) to the end of the *last person's* name, and if you have two people who own two of one type of thing, add the ('s) to the end of *each person's* name.

Example:

- Jackson and Paulie's dogs tore up my yard.

Here we see that they are both Jackson's *and* Paulie's dogs, and so we treat "Jackson and Paulie" as one entity here, putting the ('s) at the end of Paulie's name.

Contrasting that, here is another example:

- Ryan's and Michelle's cars are broken down.

Here, both Ryan and Michelle *each* have cars. They are not the same car, owned by both of them, and so we must distinguish that by adding ('s) to the end of both Ryan and Michelle. It could be broken into two sentences (i.e. "Ryan's car is broken down. Michelle's car is also broken down.") and still be comprehensible.

There is one more thing we need to look at: Possessive Personal Pronouns. These mix a little differently. When we talk about possessive pronouns, what we mean are "my" and "our". In this case, add the ('s) to the nouns that come *before* the pronoun.

Example:

- <u>Cierra</u>'s, <u>Micheal</u>'s, and <u>my</u> cats are going to the vet soon.
- The car is <u>Tyler</u>'s and <u>mine</u>.

Here we see that the Possessive Personal Pronoun comes after the other nouns, which have the ('s). This might sound a little strange on the tongue. Think of it like this: if we removed the other nouns, how would the sentence read?

- The car is ~~Tyler's and~~ mine.
- ~~Cierra's, Micheals, and~~ (M)y cats are going to the vet soon.

Phrasal Verbs

Phrasal Verbs are two or more words that act together to create a whole new verb. They are "phrases" that create verbs. You use these as well, likely on a daily basis, without even knowing it. Here are some examples:

- to break down
- to call off
- to dress up
- to fall apart
- to get away

These words combine a verb with an adverb or preposition (which acts as the **particle*** for the verb) to create an entirely new "phrasal verb". Conjugation of phrasal verbs can be difficult. Here are the rules:

- If the phrasal verb is used as the main verb in the sentence, conjugate *only* the verb portion of the phrasal verb, leaving the particle alone.
- Irregular verbs are conjugated normally (as normal as irregular verbs *can* be conjugated), again while leaving the particle alone.

Here are some examples:

<u>"to get over it"</u>

Past:
- He *got over* it.

Present:
- He *is getting over* it.

Future:
- He *will get over* it.

We see here that "over" did not change its form, even as "get" was conjugated into different forms. This is how Phrasal Verbs work. Conjugate the verb, leave the particle alone.

* A **particle** is a piece of grammar that does not change its form through inflection nor does it fit neatly into established "parts of speech" rules. If we look at some of the phrasal verbs above, we see other words act as the particle (i.e. "down", "off", "up") that almost seem to describe the verb in a non-adverbial manner.

Adverbial Sentences, Phrases, and Clauses

Adverbial Sentences

Adverbial Sentences are sentences that start with an adverb. This may seem easy to understand at a first glance. After all, starting sentences with adverbs is something we do all the time! Take a look at these two sentences:

- She crept up the stairs slowly.
- Slowly, she crept up the stairs.

The first sentence places emphasis on the action of creeping up the stairs.

The second sentence places emphasis on *how* she crept up the stairs. This can help build suspense and is good nutrition for fiction writing.

Where it gets tricky is with adverbs of time. For instance, "yesterday" is an adverb, because it modifies *when* the verb happened. Typically, one would start an adverbial phrase as I have done with this very sentence: with an adverb, and then a comma. However, with adverbs of time, this is not always necessary.

Take a look at this sentence, and then reimagine it without the comma:

- Eagerly, I started to eat.

Without the comma, the sentence feels almost rushed and unnatural. Juxtapose that with this sentence:

- Eventually I'll go to the store.

"Eventually" here is an adverb, modifying "will go". There is no comma necessary here, possibly because in speech, there wouldn't be a need for a pause.

Adverbial Phrases

Adverbial Phrases are two or more words acting together as an adverb that modifies the main clause of a sentence. They can be made up of modifying words or even two adverbs. Typically, these are created with the addition of a qualifier or intensifier to the core adverb.
Examples:

- I got to school <u>very quickly</u>.
- The cat fell off the wall <u>somewhat clumsily</u>.

Here we see that there is a word describing the adverb, which in turn describes the clause. "Very quickly" acts as an adverb to "got", but "very" modifies "quickly", which in whole modifies "got".

Adverbial Phrases also include prepositional phrases such as "in the morning" or infinitive phrases such as "to claim a prize".

Examples:

- He went to the lottery office <u>to claim a prize</u>.
- I will meet you at the park <u>in the morning</u>.

Quite peculiarly (this is also an adverbial phrase), you may notice that there are no specific adverbs in these Adverbial Phrases. In these instances, one does not need a specific adverb because the phrase *itself* acts as the adverb, modifying the verb and clause.

Here, "to claim a prize" modifies "went" as a reason, and "in the morning" modifies "meet" as a time. Common categories for Adverbial Phrases are: Manner; Place; Purpose; and Time.

We can see that going "to claim a prize" describes the purpose of the conjugated "to go" (here: went) and thus acts as the adverb. The same thing can be seen with "in the morning", describing the time of the verb "meet".

Adverbial Clauses

Adverbial Clauses are **clauses*** containing a subject and a verb that act as an adverb. Connecting these clauses to the main sentence is usually a **subordinating**

conjunction** such as "because", "if", "before", "although", and "since". These clauses are always dependent (meaning they cannot stand alone as a sentence).

Examples:

- I drove <u>as fast as I could</u>.
- She will be here soon <u>if she catches the next bus</u>.

Here we see the Adverbial Clauses of "as fast as I could" and "if she catches the next bus". In the former's case, we see that there is a subject (I) and a verb (could **(this is a modal verb***)**)) that link with the descriptor of Manner to create a descriptor for the verb "drove". In the latter, we see that the subject (she) and verb (catches/to catch) are present, with the descriptor of "the next bus" and the subordinating conjunction of "if", to create a descriptor of conditionality for "will be". There are several descriptor types for Adverbial Clauses, some of which include:

- Manner
- Place
- Purpose
- Time
- Conditionality

* A **Clause** is a group of linked words containing a subject and a verb. They can be dependent (unable to

stand alone) or independent (able to stand alone, usually with an object present).

    ** A **Subordinating Conjunction** is a word or phrase that links a dependent clause with an independent clause. Usually creates a cause-and-effect type of relationship, or it indicates that there is a shift in time between the two clauses. Typically a comma is included before the usage of a Subordinating Conjunction.

    *** A **Modal Verb** is a verb that shows possibility, intent, ability, or necessity. Think: *can, could, should,* and *must.* They are also referred to as *auxiliary verbs* (i.e. "helper verbs") because they modify the meaning of the sentence in relationship to the verb. These verbs are attached to the infinitive form of the main verb in the sentence ("I *can go* to the store" is the only way to write this sentence correctly; any other form of "to go" would be incorrect).

Garden Path Sentences

A Garden Path Sentence is a grammatically correct sentence that starts in such a manner as to confuse the reader on some aspect of the sentence. "Garden path" refers to the saying "to be led down [or up] the garden path", meaning to be deceived, tricked, or seduced. These sentences create momentary ambiguity and when read, the sentences can be perceived as grammatically incorrect or wrong due to the ambiguity.

Examples:

- The old man the boat. (This one is particularly infamous.)
- The car raced up the street flipped.
- He painted the wall with cracks.
- The girl told the story cried.

Let's make these more understandable:

- The old (people) man (as in: to staff) the boat.
- The car (that was) raced up the street flipped.
- He painted the wall (that had) cracks.
- The girl (who was) told the story cried.

The first thing one may notice when comparing

these, is that the Garden Path Sentences above use ambiguous grammar and wording. For instance, in, "The old man the boat," when we see the word *the*, followed by an adjective + noun, *old man*, we expect that the meaning refers to a singular old man because of the way we read most sentences starting with a *determiner - adjective - noun* pattern. That is to say, we expect *the* to be the article, which is a word used to define a noun, the noun being *old man*. However, 'man' here is a verb, thus leading to the confusion, as the sentence is actually structured as *determiner - noun - verb*.

We can also look at, "The car raced up the street flipped," in a similar light because again, it goes against the grain of what we usually encounter. In this instance, *raced* is a verb that could be interpreted as being in the simple past form at first, but when *flipped* is encountered, producing a doubling up on past tense verbs, the reader must look again at the sentence to determine that *car* is the object of a subordinate clause wherein *raced* is the past participle, not the verb. This again has to do with how we usually read sentences, this time being in the pattern of *agent - action - object*. "The car raced up the street flipped" is structured as *object - descriptor - action*.

Some other examples are:

- The cotton clothing is made of grows in the south.
- The man who whistles tunes piano.
- The dog that I had really loved bones.

Donkey Sentences[2]

A Donkey Sentence is a sentence whose pronoun has a clear meaning, but whose syntactical role is hard for grammarians to parse. These sentences are hard to make **well-formed*** versions of. A Donkey Pronoun, from which Donkey Sentences get their name, is the pronoun that is without a quantifier (that which denotes a set, such as every or all) or conditional (think: if, then), that nevertheless ties to a (usually) **indefinite article**** within the sentence.

This might seem like a lot, so here are some examples:

- Every farmer who owns a donkey beats it. (From which the term "Donkey Sentences" comes.)
- Every person who goes to an aquarium remembers it.

Examining that last one further, we can see that "it" is the "Donkey Pronoun", the dangling pronoun at the end. This sentence is grammatically correct. There is nothing syntactically wrong with it. However, attempting to parse it will yield strange results.

First, examine the noun "aquarium". This is what the Donkey Pronoun "it" refers to. From there, we have to

179

talk about Universal Quantifiers and Existential Quantifiers.

Universal Quantifiers, such as *given any, for all, for any*, are meant to denote that within the set of X, every individual can satisfy the requirement for the property or relation between them all. In other words, Universal Quantifiers state that all of X are similar.

Existential Quantifiers, such as *there exists, there are some, there is at least one*, are meant to denote that within a subset of X, there are some members of said subset that are A, while others are B, or C, or so on. In other words, Existential Quantifiers state that within X, there are traits that exist, but they may not all be the same.

With that out of the way, we turn our attention toward "an aquarium", which *appears to be* an Existential Quantifier (i.e. an, singular, ascribing individual traits to all aquariums despite being in the category of 'Aquariums'). Using this to attempt to translate the sentence into a more well-formed version, we arrive at the conclusion that "it" is in reference to "aquarium", meaning that every person (a Universal Quantifier present in the form of 'every') individually who goes to an aquarium (an Existential Quantifier present in the form of 'an') remembers *that* aquarium.

Breaking down logically, it looks like this:

- Every (Universal Quantifier) person (Noun) who goes to an (Existential Quantifier) aquarium (Noun) remembers (Verb) it (Pronoun).

This leaves us with an equation where:

- $\forall x$ = Universal Quantifier
- Ξx = Existential Quantifier
- ^ = a **Logical Conjunction*****
- > = a Material Implication ($P > Y$, meaning that unless Y is false, P is true)
- People = X (Noun)
- Aquarium = Y (Noun)

Utilizing these symbols to break down grammar is known as **Montague Grammar******.

So it could be translated as:

- $\forall x$ (Person(x) ^ Ξx (Aquarium(y) ^ Goes (x, y)) > Remembers (x, y))

This crazy mathematical string is just saying that if you try and parse it out like this, you will get a situation in which every person, an aquarium, and the verb goes (which affects both of the nouns) imply that both the person and aquarium remembers. This is not true, and so the y, "aquarium", is left free.

Let's try it another way:

- $\forall x$ Ξx (Person(x) ^ Aquarium(y) ^ Goes (x, y) > Remembers (x, y))

This translation is saying that y, the existential clause (i.e. an aquarium) is true for every instance of x (i.e. every person). This translation misses that it is already true if there is any object that is not an aquarium. It is saying that both every person and some people within that category as well who go to the aquarium remembers it, making the existential clause true for all of x. Where x = each and some, and Goes (x, y) > Remembers (x, y), the condition would be true for every instance of x.

Let's get it right:

- $\forall x$ $\forall y$ ((Person(x) ^ Aquarium(y) ^ Goes (x, y) > Remembers (x, y))

Here we see that by applying the properties of a Universal Quantifier where usually an Existential Quantifier would work (here meaning that "an aquarium" represents all aquariums), we get a sentence in which every aquarium that every person goes to is remembered. This indicates that indefinites (here: "an") must sometimes be interpreted as Existential Quantifiers and at other times be interpreted as Universal Quantifiers to satisfy the pronoun's predicates.

So sometimes "an" means to quantify something individually, and sometimes universally, which is what happens when we parse out the Donkey Sentence: "Every person who goes to an aquarium remembers it."

*A **well-formed** sentence is a sentence that obeys

relevant forms of grammar in its construction. The opposite of this is an ill-formed sentence, which violates traditional rules of grammar.

    ** An **indefinite article** is an article used when referring to an unspecified quantity or thing. Think: *a, an*. These articles describe ambiguity around the thing we are describing. If we say, "a lion" we are referring to a lion that we know little about - we don't know its specific name, properties, or behaviors - as opposed to saying, "*the* lion", which uses a *definite article* that displays that we know enough about a particular lion to single it out effectively.

    *** A **logical conjunction** is when the *and* of a set of variables is true *if and only if* all variables are true within the conjunction. So if we have C ^ D, and it is true, then C and D *must* be true as well.

    **** **Montague Grammar** is an approach to linguistic semantics based on mathematical logic. It is too complicated for a full explanation within this dictionary.

Comparative Illusions

A Comparative Illusion, also known as an Escher Sentence, is a sentence which initially seems grammatically acceptable, but which upon closer inspection has no well-formed or sensible meaning. This ungrammatical format stems from the usage of a **matrix clause subject*** such as *more people*, which marks a comparison between two sets of individuals. The issue with Escher Sentences is that in the latter part of the sentence, the second set, to which the first is compared, never appears.

Examples:

- More people have eaten ravioli than I have.
- More dogs have crossed the river than my dog has.

These sentences may seem acceptable at first glance, but when we examine the lack of a a **bare plural**** in the second clause, we can see how this is ungrammatical. Examine these examples, which shift the sentences' meanings to gain coherence:

- More people have eaten ravioli than I (thought (had eaten ravioli).

- More dogs have crossed the river than my dog (could have imagined (had crossed the river).

Here we see that the comparison is finally linked to something. In the first sentence, we see that *more people* is one side of the comparison, with *than I thought had eaten ravioli* being in reference to the set of people that the narrator *thought had eaten* ravioli. Thus there are two sets being compared, making the grammar correct.

The same thing occurs with the second sentence. *More dogs* is the first part of the comparison, and *than my dog could have imagined crossed the river* represents the set of dogs *thought to have* crossed the river.

When we sluff off the second part of the comparison, as was done in the first examples (i.e. More people have eaten ravioli than I have), we find the sentence compares *more people*, a set, to the singular *I*.

Some theories have evolved as to why these sentences seem grammatical, yet are not. The first involves the concept that Escher Sentences blend two grammatically correct clauses into one ungrammatical clause. See these examples:

- <u>More people</u> have eaten ravioli than I thought they had.
- Other people<u> have eaten more ravioli than I have</u>.

Combined, they turn into:

- More people have eaten ravioli than I have.

But this theory has some holes. For instance, just because each clause is correct in its original sentence, *doesn't* mean that it is acceptable in the combined sentence. Take this for example:

- <u>Stella is too short</u> to fit through the dog door.
- Stella uses the dog door as much <u>as Rogue does</u>.

Combined, they turn into:

- Stella is too short as Rogue does.

The theory goes deeper. It can be said that the first and second sentence, from which the clauses are pulled, must have a similar lexical element to them. However, this requires, for the Comparative Illusion to manifest, that the second sentence of the three would be ungrammatical.

Look at these examples:

- <u>More dogs have crossed the river</u> than my dog had thought.
- Dogs have crossed the river more <u>than my dog has.</u>

Combined, they turn into:

- More dogs have crossed the river than my dog has.

The second theory has to do with **ellipsis***** and how it interacts with the sentence. This is called the Repair-By-Ellipsis hypothesis. This suggests that sentences with ellipsis will be judged as more acceptable than those without ellipsis. The theory goes that the 'unsaid' part of the sentence resolves the obscure hangup between the comparatives.

Here is an example:

- More people have been to Europe than I have [been to Greece].

Take this sentence into account for a moment. Suppose it makes less sense; it would then support the idea that without the ellipsis [been to Greece] the sentence would be more sensible. If, however, it makes the same amount of sense, then it could be reasoned that the Repair-By-Ellipsis theory doesn't quite work because it still does not explain how the sentence reads acceptably. Consider that even if we repeated the phrase, "...have been to Europe..." the sentence still wouldn't quite make sense.

- More people have been to Europe than I have [been to Europe].

Because of the repetition, this one is likely to be judged as being less comprehensible.

The third theory is all about the ambiguity of the word *more*. There are two ways to use the word *more*: in the additive sense, and in the comparative sense. Consider the sentences:

- Abby worked on the project for ten hours, and still had to work more.
- I worked on the project more than Collin did.

Here we see the word *more* used in two distinct senses. In the first sentence, *more* is representing an additive quality, in the sense that Abby must work some quantity in addition to the hours she has already worked, perhaps more, perhaps less than ten hours. In the second sentence, we see that the word *more* is comparing the amount of work I did to the amount of work Collin did.

When we talk about Comparative Illusions, the *more* present *must* be used in the comparative sense. The additive is nearly unavailable, as, when it is said, "More people have been to Europe than I have," it cannot be stated that more people, as in *more* than have already gone, have gone to Europe because of the existence of the *than* clause that connects that *more* the second part of the sentence.

However, it *can* be confused for an additive *more* at first, and here is where the confusion is hypothesized.

This is called the Additive *More* hypothesis.

This theory hinges on the idea that the Comparative Illusion effect should be possible only when an additive semantics for *more* is supported. Firstly, it must be possible, within this hypothesis, for the subject of the *than* clause to fit the matrix subject so that the additive *more* can work here. However, if we have a sentence where the matrix subject and the *than* clause subject can *not* align, we have a problem. Consider this example:

- More dogs have eaten kibble than that cat has.

Assuming no cat belongs to the set of dogs, this sentence cannot mean, "More dogs have eaten kibble than [just that one] cat has." This is because, in order for the *more* to be additive, both sets must be the same as to add to the set requires that the set is in congruence.

This theory has two assumptions: one, that, "More dogs have eaten kibble than that cat has" will be interpreted as less acceptable than "More people have been to Europe than I have" due to the incongruence between the subject sets; and two, that flipping *more* for *fewer* (i.e. "Fewer people have been to Europe than I have") should be less acceptable because the additive quality (or subtractive quality) fails to uphold the additive semantics of *more*.

And finally, there is the event comparison theory.

This has to do with the way we compare events and quantities. For instance, it is grammatical to say this example:

- People have been to Berlin more than I have.

It is possible that the Comparative Illusion effect stems from people analyzing the following example as the one proposed before:

- More people have been to Berlin than I have.

However, it is also possible to interpret numerically-quantified noun and noun phrases as expressing the count of individual participation in the event. Look at *more people* and examine that there is the potential for it to quantify ambiguously that a number of people greater than one (i.e. *I*) has been to Berlin. At the same time, it is possible to read it as an expression of individual participation, which is to say that: *more (individuals) have been to Berlin than (one individual) has*. Let's break it into examples, starting by examining the fleshing out of a numerically-quantified sentence and then exploring the implications, for easier viewing:

- Ten people have been to Berlin ten times each, and one individual went to Berlin fifty times.

Here we have a grammatically correct sentence,

one that is numerically quantified as shown by *ten people, ten times*, and so on. Now, we examine this Comparative Illusion:

- More people have been to Berlin than I have.

This sentence is *true* if and only if we count individual participation. This means that we count *ten people* as having gone *ten times*, which is more than *one individual* having gone *fifty times*. The important parts are the nouns (i.e. how many people have been to Berlin). This means that 10 is greater than 1, thus making the sentence true.

However, if we consider the events, we get a different result. In this case, *ten people* have gone *ten times*, but *one individual* went *fifty times*. With the emphasis on the events, we see that 10 is not greater than 50, thus making the sentence false.

The event comparison reading is maintained because it is grammatically allowed by the subject matrix clause, and persists despite not being supported upon reaching the *than* clause.

*A **matrix clause subject** is the subject of the clause in a sentence which contains another clause. Think: (often) *main clause* and *dependent clause*. The matrix clause subject can also be a subordinate clause, or contain the subordinate clause within it. An example is:

- She told her friend that the man who robbed her had had a bruise.

Here, the matrix clause is *the man ... had had a bruise*, and within that, we find the subordinate clause *who robbed her*. We can rethink of the sentence like this, for clarity:

- <u>The man</u>, who robbed her, <u>had had a bruise</u>, and she told her friend.

Here we see a combination of clauses, both *the man had had a bruise* and *who robbed her*, which is the subordinating clause within the matrix clause. The matrix clause contains the most important information. A subordinating clause is a clause that is somehow less important than the main, more important clause.

    ** A **bare plural** is the plural of a bare noun, which is a noun without a surface quantifier or determiner. Think: *<u>dogs</u> bark*; *<u>cats</u> are common*; *he is at <u>sea</u>*. These nouns have no quantification or determiner (also known as a limiting adjective, which is a word that appears before a noun to give us more context about the noun), and are thus said to be bare. There are several complexities around bare plurals.

    *** An **ellipsis** is an omission within speech, often common and understood despite the lacking parts of grammar. Think: *have everything*? Here, grammatically speaking, the sentence *should* read: *do you have* *everything*? Here, we omit [do you] because it is understood, and thus becomes the ellipsis.

Center Embedding

Center Embedding is the process of embedding a phrase within another phrase of the same type. This leads to difficulty parsing the sentence, and makes grammatical analysis difficult. Most frequently, this is exemplified through embedding a **relative clause*** inside another relative clause.

Example:

- The girl that the boy knows ate the apple.

Here, the relative clause embedded within another clause is "that the boy knows", which is centered within "the girl … ate the apple". This is sensible; however, if we add *another* relative clause, it becomes less so.

Example:

- The girl that the boy that the woman knows ate the apple.

We could, theoretically, extend this indefinitely.

- The girl that the boy that the woman that the man that the dog [etcetera] knows ate the apple.

But as we add more and more relative clauses to it, it becomes *much* harder to make sense of, both as we read it, and as we parse it grammatically. Let's break down why.

To start, let's look at embedding. This refers to any subordinating clause relating to a main clause. In other words, a clause is *embedded* within the main clause, and can be multiple times. The three type of sub-clauses are:

1. Complement: a clause used as a complement for another word, specifically (typically) as it relates to a verb, adjective, or noun.
2. Relative: the main type of clause we are looking at for Center Embedding (see the definition below).
3. Adverbial: a dependent clause that functions as an adverb.

Center Embedding contains words from the main clause on both sides of the sub-clauses. Multiple Center Embedding of the same *type* of clause is referred to as self-embedding. A Center Embedded clause that is a self-embedded relative clause looks like the sentences in the examples above (i.e. the girl that the boy…).

One can End Embed a sentence too. See this example:

*   She never knew he had thought she had seen that he went to the church.

This is a complementing End Embedded sentence. The verb, *expected*, is complemented by *he had thought*, which in turn is complemented by *she had seen* and so on. Think of it like this:

- <u>She never knew</u> [he had thought [she had seen]] <u>that he went to church.</u>

In other words, we have a simple sentence (i.e. She never knew that he went to church), and within that, we have added two complementary clauses, namely: [that he had thought]; and [that she had seen]. Both of these complement a proceeding word, and we can see, when the sentence is broken down, that it truly has meaning. See this:

- She never knew that he went to church, but he thought she had seen him [go to church].

This is a much more understandable sentence, but thanks to End Embedding the clauses, the original example is also parsable. This differs from Center Embedding.

So why is Center Embedding almost impossible to parse after a point? Well, it has to do with the limitations of the human short term memory! It is one thing to embed at the end of a clause (i.e. [he had thought[she had seen]]) because it follows a natural progression within the sentence. In the center, however, we get a sentence that looks like this:

- The sandwich that the boy that the girl liked made tasted great.

…that gets parsed like this:

- The sandwich [...] tasted great.
- The sandwich [that the boy [...] made] tasted great.
- The sandwich [that the boy [that the girl liked] made] tasted great.

Therein lies the issue, despite no grammatical rules being broken. The Center Embedded clause *that the girl liked* is surrounded by *that the boy ... made*, and herein we see that confusion can arise from losing track of who made, tasted, and liked. To understand this sentence, one must both understand the relative clause that is currently unfolding, while also remembering the subject matrix clause of the whole sentence, and comprehending how the two tie together, all at the same time. The more clauses there are, the more there is to remember and logically conjugate in your mind.

    * A **relative clause** is a clause that modifies a noun or noun phrase and which uses a grammatical device (pronoun, modifier, etcetera) to denote that the

clause refers to the noun or noun phrase. In other words, a relative clause is a clause relating to another clause via a linking grammatical device.

Split Infinitives

Split Infinitives might seem easy to understand at first. There is no easy way to dive into the depths of Split Infinitives without busting through that ease, so to start, let's define an infinitive.

An infinitive can be thought of as the "to" version of a verb. It is the **uninflected*** form of a verb, which can also act as an adjective or adverb as well as a gerund. An example of an infinitive as a noun is:

- The only choice I have is *to run*.
- One sometimes has *to eat* something they don't want to.
- The best hope we have is *to forgive*.

Here, the infinitive acts as a gerund. But what about when infinitives act as adverbs or adjectives? Well, we could get sentences like this:

- I displayed a willingness *to help*.
- Sometimes people don't care *to understand*.

The first example here utilizes the infinitive as an adjective, modifying the noun *willingness*. In the second, *to understand* modifies the verb *care*, making it an adverb. Seems simple so far, most likely.

So let's split them.

Look at this example:

- In order *to **fully** understand,* we must go where no man has gone before.
- We knew that our best chance was *to **completely and utterly** destroy* them.

This illustrates the Split Infinitive, which is an infinitive that is "split" by an adverb or adverbial phrase. There are a few rules (more like suggestions and encouragements) around splitting an infinitive, which is where it gets more dicey.

When moving the adverb or adverbial phrase to the end of the phrase *doesn't* change the meaning of the sentence, one should try to keep the infinitive in tact. When it *does* change the meaning of the sentence, one should split the infinitive. Look at these examples to see where splitting the infinitive doesn't change the meaning:

- He urged me *to **gradually** approach* the topic in class.
- He urged me *to approach* the topic **gradually** in class.

Here we can see the "split", *gradually*, when moved, does not change the meaning of the sentence. Here, the second sentence is preferred. We also don't want to split infinitives too widely, like in this example:

- This program allows your child *to **easily, gently, and confidently** acclimate* to the swimming pool.

In this example, we've created too wide a gulf in the infinitive, when we could have also said:

- This program allows your child *to acclimate* to the swimming pool **easily, gently, and confidently**.

It is apparent that moving the adverb or adverbial phrase around in the sentence keeps the meaning of the sentence in tact. To contrast with these, examine this example:

- These items are expected *to **rapidly** go up* in price to about seventy dollars.

Go ahead and try moving the adverbial phrase around in the sentence. You likely won't be able to without shifting the meaning or making it awkward, confusing, or nonsensical. We can't cleanly say, for instance:

- These items are expected **rapidly** *to go up*…
- These items are expected *to go up* in price **rapidly** to…

Technically, there is nothing ungrammatical about shifting the adverb. It's more about the vibes of the sentence, and what makes the most naturalistic sense to the reader with the least confusion attached. Because there is ambiguity when the word *rapidly* is shifted, it is best to keep the infinitive split to ensure that the emphasis on how quickly the price will *go up* is maintained.

One more example is:

- The company plans *to **more than** quadruple* their sales numbers.

Try moving *more than* around in the sentence and see for yourself why that infinitive is split!

* **Inflection** is the changing of the form of a word to express a particular grammatical function or attribute (think: tense, mood, person, number, gender). If you change *to go* to *have gone*, you've inflected the verb to past tense. If you change *a dog* to *dogs*, you have inflected that word to represent multiple dogs.

Adjective Order

This is likely the oddest rule in the Dictionary. You use it *every day*, and drive the sentences that utilize it with vibes alone. It's hardly taught, and hardly consciously thought about in grammatical formation. Moreso, adjective order just "feels right", despite having a complex rule lurking beneath the vibes. See this example to start:

- She wore an interesting blue shirt today.

  Sounds right, right? What about this one:

- She wore a blue interesting shirt today.

This one sounds wrong, right? Well, there's a reason for it, and it's actually pretty simple and concrete. Though a bit obscure, once broken down, we see that adjectives really do have an order, and that order is:

1. Opinion: the opinion of the narrator.
2. Size: the size of the noun.
3. Physical Quality: the qualities of the noun *besides* the qualities listed here (think: *untidy, rough, thick*).

4. Shape: the literal shape of the noun (think: round, square, octagonal).
5. Age: the age descriptor of the noun.
6. Color: the color of the noun.
7. Origin: where the noun originates from.
8. Material: what the noun is made of.
9. Type: the classification of the noun (think: *general-purpose, three-sided, upside-down*).
10. Purpose: what the noun does (think: *cleaning, cooking, fixing*).

Let's write a complete sentence utilizing the complete list:

- The grungy, oversized, thick, square, ancient blue Turkish fabric welcoming entrance rug smelled foul.

This sentence literally goes in order of 1, 2, 3, 4, and so on, and thus it sounds grammatically correct. Shifting it around to look like this:

- The oversized, square, grungy, blue, ancient, Turkish welcoming fabric entrance rug smelled foul.

…sounds terribly wrong *only* because it does not follow the natural order of adjectives. So why *are* adjectives ordered like this? Well, we don't really know. Some theories state it has to do with how close the adjectives are to the noun, and what that says about their importance in relation to the noun. This doesn't always hold up, however, as some adjectives are of equal importance to contextualizing the noun.

Elsewise, we look to the semantics of the adjectives to surmise their order, though phonological (i.e. literal speech patterns) and pragmatic (i.e. idioms, emphasis, etc) factors are thought to play a role too. Still, no one *really* agrees why these factors make us order our adjectives like this. It is, oddly, still a linguistic mystery.

Syllepsis versus Zeugma

Syllepsis and Zeugma sound like made up words, so we need to define them right at the start of this section.

- To be in *Syllepsis* means that the governing word of a clause has two different and distinct relations with the "governed" words, *specifically* <u>grammatically</u>.
- To be in *Zeugma* means that the logic and <u>semantics</u> between the governing word and the two modified words is different.

This might sound *very* similar, and some argue they are the same thing. But let's break it down a bit.

A Syllepsis looks like this:

- He caught the bus, and a bad cold.
  Or:
- Neither they nor it is working.

A Zeugma looks like this:

- Jacob and his permit expired last week.
  Or:
- With weeping eyes and hearts, we went to the boardwalk.

We can see the similarities. In "He caught the bus, and a bad cold." we can observe that the governing word, *caught*, refers to the bus and a bad cold in different ways. But then, in "Jacob and his permit expired last week", we can observe that the governing word, *expired*, refers to both Jacob and his permit in different ways as well. The difference is more starkly illuminated in the second examples.

"Neither they nor it is working." exemplifies that the governing word, *working*, refers to they and it in different grammatical senses. For example, writing, "it is working" is grammatically correct, but "they is working" is *not*. While one part of the sentence is correct, the other part is not, because the governing word interacts differently with different parts of the sentence.

Compare this to the zeugma, "With weeping eyes and hearts, we went to the boardwalk," wherein the governing word, this time the word *weeping* which applies to *eyes* and *hearts* in separate semantical manners. "*Weeping eyes*" can be taken literally, as in crying, but "*weeping hearts*" cannot be taken literally, and must be assumed to be metaphorical in nature. This is the semantic difference between the relation of the governing word and the governed words in a Zeugma.

Parataxis, Asyndeton, and Polysyndeton

Again, we immediately need to define these three terms, with the caveat that Asyndeton and Polysyndeton can represent two forms of Parataxis, while still being distinct.

- Parataxis is a figure of speech in which words, phrases, clauses, or sentences are set next to each other so that each element is equally important.
- Asyndeton is the omission of **coordinating conjunctions*** where one would normally expect them, which can represent asyndetic parataxis.
- Polysyndeton is an over-abundance of coordinating conjunctions within a sentence, which can represent syndetic parataxis.

This might all seem confusing, but there is a very, very well known example of Parataxis in our lexicon.

- Vini, Vidi, Vici. (I came, I saw, I conquered.)

We can see that each element of the sentence is equally as important as the next. Here is another example:

- The brave. The bold. The invincible.

Makes sense so far, right? Let's take a look a the two types of Parataxis now, which is where we will jump into Asyndeton and Polysyndeton. Parataxis can occur with conjunctions, but only if the specific elements of the sentence *other than the conjunction* all carry the same weight. So far we've seen one example of asyndetic parataxis, i.e. Asyndeton, in the form of "Vini, Vidi, Vici." Let's take a look at an example of syndetic parataxis, i.e. Polysyndeton.

- I went to the store and I bought all my food and I got in my car and I started to go home.

Here we see the use of *coordinating* conjunctions which allow for each piece of the sentence to carry its own equally important weight. *Subordinating* conjunctions cannot be used, as they indicate that different parts of the sentence carry different weight, which is by definition not Parataxis.

    * A **Coordinating Conjunction** is a conjunction that creates an equal relationship with different parts of the sentence. This is the opposite of a subordinating conjunction, which denotes which parts of the sentence are more important than others.

Miscellaneous Obscurities

The Interrobang

The Interrobang is a symbol that is a mix of the exclamation point (!) and the question mark (?). It looks like: ‽. Have you ever seen a sentence end with a (!?)? ‽ is the **ligatured*** version of (!?). It is an expression of an exclamatory question, and is usually seen written out fully rather than in its ligatured version.

The Interrobang first appeared in 1962, proposed by Martin K. Speckter, an American advertising agent who surmised that advertisements would look better if (!?) could be condensed into one mark (see: ligatured). He chose the name *interrobang* as a reference to the marks that inspired the punctuation, namely being: *interrogatio*, Latin for "rhetorical question" or "cross-examination"; and *bang*, printers' slang for the exclamation mark.

* **Ligaturing** is when two symbols are combined into one symbol.

Good-bye

Did you know that "goodbye" is a contraction? Originally, "goodbye", when uncontracted, meant "God be with ye". God be with ye > Godbe withye > Goodbye. So when you tell someone goodbye, you're really telling them to go with God!

This isn't the only word like this. Think of the word "ampersand". This is a contraction of "and per se and", which is why & means "and".

Compound Plurals

Some nouns, when pluralized, place the 's' in the *middle* of the word, rather than at the end. Think of the word "passerby". The plural is "passer(s)by", instead of "passerbys" or, worse, "passerbies". This happens commonly with Compound Plurals, which is a plural formed by compounding two words (in this case, passers and by). We could also do this for the word:

So why does this happen? Well, with *passersby*, we have a noun + a preposition, thus forming the whole word (i.e. (n.) passer, (p.) by). Here, we pluralize the *noun*, not the preposition. This is called a Compound Noun.

However, if we create a Compound *Verb*, such as buildup, where we have a verb + a preposition, we add the 's' to the *end*. So "buildup" becomes "buildups".

There are caveats, though.

For instance, we don't say "rainsforest". We say "rainforests". Why? Well, because "rainforest" is considered *one word* despite being a compounding of two words. We wouldn't hyphenate it, because breaking the word is unnecessary. There is no preposition, but rather, a verb + noun to form the new word.

However, with *passersby*, we *can* hyphenate it (to passers-by). This is because we have a **Principle Noun*** and a complementary preposition that finishes the meaning. In "passerby"/"passer-by", we have a principle word (i.e. passer) and the preposition, which finishes the meaning of the word (i.e. by, which describes the noun "passer"). This is dependent on the presence of the preposition that describes a noun.

So the *only* time we pluralize in the middle of the word is when we have a noun + preposition formula within the word. See these examples:

- Hanger-on > Hangers-on
- Sister-in-Law > Sisters-in-Law

Now look at the plurals for a verb + preposition formula:

- Walk-in > Walk-ins
- Take-out > Take-outs

* A **Principle Word** is the main word within a compound word. Think: *walk*-ins, *hanger*-on, and *take*-outs.

Imperative Sentences with Implied Subjects

An Imperative Sentence is a sentence that gives an order, command, or instructions to the subject, typically beginning with a verb. The subject is often implied and thus ellipsed (remember: ellipsis is when part of the sentence is implied rather than said). This leads to the shortest sentence in the English language:

"Go."

Here, the subject is ellipsed. The subject could be "you", or "they", or even "we", but it is ellipsed and context dependent. The imperative then remains. This is because the subject of this type of sentence is often the audience being directly addressed. In other words, saying "Go!" as a command or instruction is often directed at the audience of the sentence, which makes the presence of a subject redundant.

Let's look at another example:

- Throw that away.

Here, the implied subject is the audience (i.e. "You" throw that away). We see the sentence starts with a verb, commanding the subject, here the audience, to do something.

The subject isn't always implied in imperative sentences. An example of this is:

- Bring me the paper, Sarah.

It is still an imperative sentence (starting with a verb (i.e "bring")) but the subject is present at the end of the sentence.

One can also use adverbs or modifiers/descriptors as the first word, immediately followed by the imperative verb. For instance, we would do this for politeness, such as:

- Please take out the trash.

Or we can do this to describe *how* we would like the imperative to be done, such as:

- Quickly run upstairs and grab my suitcase.

In these instances, there is a modifying word + an imperative verb, often with an ellipsed subject.

Addendum

Addendum

1: Superscript U's indicate either unique words or words whose synonyms are in their definition.

2: A lot of my understanding of Donkey Sentences comes from Wikipedia and the sources within it. Donkey pronouns and sentences are real, but rarely talked about it seems. If you check the Wikipedia page for Donkey Sentences, you'll see a similar sentence broken down in a similar manner. I did my best to make it understandable for this dictionary, and apologize if I have failed to do so.

3. The *Dictionary of Obscure Sorrows* produced the word "Sonder". It is by and large my favorite word, which is why I included it here. I encourage every reader of this dictionary to purchase a copy of the *Dictionary of Obscure Sorrows*. Some of the most fantastic words I've ever encountered come from this book.